LURE

LURE

NILS MICHALS

Lena-Miles Wever Todd Poetry Series
PLEIADES PRESS
Warrensburg, Missouri
& Rock Hill, South Carolina

Published by Pleiades Press
Department of English & Philosophy
Central Missouri State University
Warrensburg, Missouri 64093
&
Department of English
Winthrop University
Rock Hill, SC 29733

Distributed by Louisiana State University Press

2 4 6 8 9 7 5 3 1
First Pleiades Press Printing, 2004

On the cover:
"Bearing Fruit" by Michael Crespo
oil/linen 34"X24"
Courtesy of the artist, Michael Crespo, and David Lusk Gallery

Grateful acknowledgement is due to the following publications in which some of these poems, or versions thereof, originally appeared:

Beloit Poetry Journal—"The Ambulance Came & We Know How That Goes"

Can We Have Our Ball Back?— "Aloha" and "Prayer"

Cutbank—The Stone Letters: "If there the studio fire should blue," "In answer to your answer: Yes" and "Today a Blue, throat and fluke in the dock hoist"

Faultline—"After Surgery," "Lesser Season (II)" and "Lesser Season (III)"

Indiana Review—"Revolving Around Tycho Brahe: Wenceslas Square" and "Stradivari, 1736"

jubilat:—"Westerly"

Pleiades: "Desperation Series"

"Westerly" also appeared as a special edition from the Underwood Broadside Series.

Special thanks to Patricia Goedicke, Judy Jordan, Joanna Klink, Cole Swensen, family, friends, and colleagues.

CONTENTS

Though it come to the last,
I shall still go before thee thy pilot.

—Herman Melville

Westerly

What comes off the sea recalls nothing
of loving a world and for those with eyes
wishing something other than what is seen
it says: listen.
Comes off the sea and does not care, says accept
there may or may not be a hand
in this: a taste of spray,
salt, some origin no longer
encompassing us with calm, says
you are on your own now.
And the shy-grown citizens. City of harbors.
What comes off the sea has tinned the sea
wide and for miles like wheat blown one direction.
Off the sea, the distance it has glassed
faltering, comes near to ask
Who are you, and after you answer,
just sea, air,
nowhere in the giftbearing world a voice
having said salt, water—
and in not saying, not a thing we may call quiet,
no voice having sung.

Revolving Around Tycho Brahe: Wenceslas Square

Waking, a woman who ate a boiled egg in bed
last night sees the snow whitening the red slopes

of churches, and once in the mirror, thinks she has been
sleepwalking in the square, removes a flake of eggshell

from her hair. The astronomical clock sputters its wood birds
to life, the metro opens its bright slant down to trains.

Hawkers unlock their chests of flashy jewels, rock
foot to foot in the cold, faces buried in steaming wine.

Swaddled in blankets, a baby is just its face,
pale and moonish. Umbrellas, bright aimless pinwheels,

drift in the passing carriages, horse musk, white clouds
pluming from nostrils like twin nebulas, cold gas and dust,

mere ingredients. Few remember where on the bridge
a man set fire to himself in '68, sat still as one

in the row of black saints petrified on the bridge,
and burned, smoking like damp wood, a grey root to the sky.

Now, the prostitutes wander home, their lioness moves, night coos
silent, breath like empty champagne flutes.

The hawks hover their fakes like moody, bearded planets
as the cobble under snow blooms in liverish spots.

The baby is too old for itself.
No magnesium flash, no alchemy, everywhere a universe

eaten by wind, nothing here center to its dying.
Did Brahe burn . . . like the man, quieter than his flames?

Did he dream of his missing nose, daydream his lover breaking
the red seal on the envelope, bond white, corners crisp,

full of bees that died stinging the dark?
Snow cannot settle on the Tyn's dim antennas,

twin spires that carry down to him
within the floors, the square spinning with those

who find the earth too vast to be anything
but the heavens vanished. Whether earth or sun,

sun or earth, somewhere a body nears the end
of its one revolution as night's thin shell of snow

vanishes, as the woman removes with difficulty
the pearled slivers from her hair.

Stradivari, 1736

Vulned, it beats, my deus, my secret
machine. And being what happens helplessly,
falls, boats the air, the angelica—
nothing more.
They snow the shop floor blind, anklefuls,
silencing footfall, corkscrewing in blocks of sun—
how light and illiterate with glee they settle. They rest
for one another. They might touch into fire.
Bergonzi has left. Damn him parading
like a fresh washed sleeve, his ruler
that unfolds like a bird.
So I've slipped in the last
thin rib. You see? And for what?
Some ruffle, some gawk, wrists polished boyishly . . .
whose prodigy? And then?
Did she startle?
They lift clean and look back, some reach
themselves. They will be swept
this evening, as evening will, vespers, and when
the bow touches there is someone
who accepts as light will an open door,
who enters, voices of others
deep within, curtained and interior the shush
of robes moving, blood coursing, cells beautifully
dividing in the dark so long against their will,
the sweet head dims
in he who lowers, falls,
a sound now on its way,
the bow touches, faint smoke
only, touches who kneels, who cannot pray, who leans
hard against all his angels.

Diodic

1

A chariot the wind is.
Brings coastal. So that on frescoes
mothwings bow.

                   Closely down the long arcades,

shade.
             Brings news of rain
so that more urgently the rotundas spit
dust and noise, peopled things clamoring for their homes
and where an opening, vespas stretching into a higher gear.
Luckful, those who ride them.

2

Keats lilting, snookered on opium.
Same wind, charioted.   *An informant,*
Joseph says. Coastal, something of olives soured,
somewhere heavy sea.
Joseph, what is that sound out of doors?
              The leaves.

No, deeper, more full.
              The wind, flooding the ruins.

No, more still, more caged.
              John, I haven't the faintest . . .

3

Powder, the sky. Waveless and precise
and not often crossed, the sky. Installed
nearly. Sky? The noun is washed
when someone is woken from sleep by their own laughter.
Having slipped from a breast pocket, his odes,
heat blonding the turned pages, all the yard's waving grasses.
Lab's collar could be warm keys at the neighbor's lock.
And the elm's leaves dissolving, silkworms,

the sound of which approaches snowfall
and wings, gently disastering things that build back
up after so long a heat and what moves
is in crisis, what moves, the contrail or the blue,
item or air—
indeed, what wouldn't allow itself untold
now that all that is harsh turns silk
rippling and the song of all this listening might pay off
as surely as the contrail's softened alluvium
is what's left of a lifted rescue—
could be the smoke of John's body
departing, could be what becomes of weather when graphed
after the quiet ardor of an eye's following—

                                And then, fled
is that music.

4

Joseph, that sound again.
                    It is raining.
So much softer than possible
for rain.
                Mist then. Here now John, some laudanum.
When they should meet which collects the other,
dust or mist?
                Dust some, mist some.
Into a handkerchief his coughs flower a more vehement red.
If only construed in oil thinks Joseph.
Joseph, that sound—
                John you mustn't rise
                    you mustn't rise
until floated across the study his hands at the mantle appear they
will never adjust to brick, there a bottled ship which is to glass
as a ship is to sky, his ear drawing near—
How mild to appear so still!
Aloft the crow's nest
oftimes calm sound of what is to pass—
the monsters in their sleep circulating in deep,
wide O unharnessable sea
and above, birds, terribly

colored birds, macaws flying north by a northstar light,
rhythmed skritterings, slumps of rigging
and the sails' starward billows in unclouded night—
tell me, song, and swiftly, between heaven and earth
do I wake or sleep?

5

At dawn a cold . . . steam whitens just off the stack's flue,
the instant of blue between them
magnetic.
                              Having been passed through in the night,
the city awakens. Frescoes washed, frosted grass. On doorsteps
coat buttons hook speechlessly. Shopdoors clatter as they roll
up, and in the pause before fruits are uncovered,
a keeper's low whistle.

Was the same wind, charioted. Gone.
Replaced.
Clean crisp still air—
                              Voltage

to light.

Desperation Series

Say not "the desperate fields." Such, and the instant it's through

Fields shed themselves massively at once. There is counterfleeting.

And wind, the future of itself just lays out. There is quiet snapping.

There is calculable loss. A woman and a man lay down in each and come

Up three. Their driftings will it, the gently forced spot, over it clouds roll.

How could the farmer even know or care now that he must ranch

Peacocks to stay alive? Say that one can hear them, say

"Say it and it shall be so," the sound moving at the level of the wheat

Gutteral and solicitous so that whatever it touches tries to silo

In what it once lost. What moves on what or whom without recompense—

Abandoned plow at the milliontipped edge, diseases in the wheat.

Nothing gets to go on forever. Say not, "one gives terribly, another trespasses too

Violently." A woman and a man, the shape of them

Pressed into the fields, over which clouds catch so still

All likening fails. Sky.

Silo. Tree. Plow. Fields. Nothing can ever hear us now say the fields.

Desperation Series

He finds the turning out of debris.

Huge tree pieces, bits of sealife.

Others at the seawall watch. Birds seem swingable against themselves.

Force as a clear moving field.

A caught charter can't power out. Oil and smoke as from taking on
water like air. The clouds in cahoots with the sea
the sea in cahoots with the jetty
                                                    the sea with itself.

There are kelp masses slung on the roads. Birds invisibly tethered
as to a floating stop.

He hears murmurs, oohs and aahs from the gallery, occasional
what a shame.

He feels the outermost of need as so near laughable, as a circumference
loosely attached and explosive.

The sea wants through, the sea with its pendulum attractors, happenstances,
the charter plowing in loops,
momentary impasse
                    wave and rock and wood giving, the sickening division.

This is debris
this is not
or whether of confluence
he can no longer with certainty say.

A bird or a piece of jacket in the bare branches. Some black smoke cartwheels
by it and is gone.

Desperation Series

From a distance so seeming it had been of another country that once
up into the looted hills so foreign was the mineral quiet

machines having once passed through here and the air less
as with some valency and ability to sieve I

could make out glittery households their meted out livings rails fractured
out the mountain dangerous electrics pools more inert in the moon's light

you said please do not look at me you are looking at me
each then was its own and listening how deeply in the shafts' slow intake

of air traversed the pitched divination rods such listening turned abusive
as that great buck kicking up rocks as a response to need

would I call this "reprieve" what would I call this space opened
not as in a room as in a house as in a woman and a man lay down

this was a kind of space not lightly toyed with a bird expires in this
one must have a constant eye for this I could not see what was taken

from here though inside there was forged breadth to move veined hidden
air was blood I saw it a body in there and felt through this place touched

so freely it had given its consent to break it.

After Surgery

Cloudbreak, the window cool with lake air,
lush passes of shade
where the sun breaks into streaking pearl,
where the shamrocks, insistent for glass,
crane for a small plain of light.
By evening I think I hear
the little closings of their three wings,
of fog simply replacing air.
Evening, hear the boats nudge
in the docks like stabled animals,
hear a pool of water where thousands
of stamp-size maple leaves
form, scatter, and form again:
star, flake, handprint.

What comes back is the open gown
breezy through rooms, prep rooms
wide and low with worry, scattered
dissimilar hands flittering
like small, self-involved birds,
mouthless mint green faces,
the lidocaine working with intelligence.
Above the I.V. drip the light,
every silver instrument lifted shadowless
from its groove, the growing
alone beneath the mask,
anesthesia, my involuntary lyric—

Evening disintegrates in frames
arrested, a red chariot that unpins
helplessly outside itself, the wheel
a windmilling O with its own mind for glory.
Someone walks light-heeled up the path,
reconsiders.
At the point of glass, an arrangement, flawless.
Darkness drops clickless over the lake,

a light patter of fog dripping
from lake pines on the skylight—
what happens to the man
who remembers the outlines of boats
in fog, then only fog—

Southerly

Comes a ship, sailors brightening the decks.
Movement. The creak and lean.
In the cobbled streets a cutpurse slows,
market dogs stall above a feast,
the queen more royally boned
than ever, her anchored silks waving
whole pageantries to a ground halt.
Comes a ship, there a sailor fascinated
with the inlay, a disc of salt in the soft part
under his eye.
That implicit leap which is sudden light,
on the sea line a bead of far clear light—
his eyes must pass on to other eyes
until a wing spans between,
though he may be mistaken and a light breeze
undoes a hull to the sky.

The Stone Letters

To Pygmalion, Master Sculptor, Court of Catherine:

If there the studio fire should blue
up the marble like a slant of weather,
if your chisel passes through
dust, bits of porphyry, early air
fogging the gold—
you might press an iris
into a map of Siberian rainfall.
You may arrange the remains
of last night's delicacy in the freshened snow.

And nightly, moths into the hanging pans' light.
Stalled above seahorses, their beds of finecrush ice,
I am the gifted mimic.
My blank palms leave such glassy distaste!
If shells should feel themselves interior,
that wine-dark,
if seasalt should flour the body's case,
hands roused, the eyes windlashed and tinned—
what have you seen? Still bell
in custody to the velvet rope unnoted
by a distant boudoir. Who keeps you?
That I do not simply die (her lofted rooms),
that I do not slip (iced eaves
the city distance), that I
(cool where the chisel touched) do not—

Galatea,

In answer to your answer: Yes.
At first light, snow, absorbed, wanting to fall just so.
Then the silver service, eggcups in the pose of swans.
Some sugared things, and at last the fine-particled studio
air, the slab's volcanic light and Russia full of scarlatines,
stork-waisted, wishing themselves marble.
They drag their foot scarves through tool dust.
They drop their ermine trains with such
performed privacy . . . Night is when Ivan
the Terrible whistles through his teeth
for Posnik Yakovlev. In question to your question:
perhaps the wind perceives most clearly?
Think of bulbed churches
foiled in gold, faded in the wind's fits.
A counterfeit flicker seems to say
St. Basil's when near, its nine cupolas'
bright applause hiding the city's fever,
so that peasant women, their minds turned pure sail,
open. Who can argue?
They move on, unmoored,
and fade among the market canopies.
Voices, a voice paling in my
ear: your name,
the name they cloud
into my looking glass,
semivowel that is snowlight.

Pygmalion,

Today a Blue, throat and fluke in the dock hoist.
A pose, flash smoke, and the wharfhands mill

about the planks, caps askew and slapping backs
until I watch no more, spyglass to the outermost

house beneath the sweep of lighthouse,
the breakers, evening's mirror as the grunion

beach in silver sheets and further, darker,
groupers play the angles. Before a field

clear and shifting, before a krillstorm, those overlit
soirees of annoyed hips and swallowtail waiters

where anemone bloom like amnesia.
My shutter, my shutter, the compass needles for an iceberg,

as the sea pulls the boys, tan and full of mackerel,
the boys drifting for my window with their handfuls

of pebbles. And through a window at evening, distant
and tinnish, at last reaching me, the swing of scythes . . .

On blacker dreams, on unending autobiographies,
on appropriate ghosts tacking through ballrooms

untouched, I give nothing, take not a thing,
the deaf spyglass obsessing the tense

and slack of slipknots at the boatslip, a boat slipping
beneath the telescope's sail.

Galatea,

Let the room's enlightened heads and shadowless gems,
fresh-chilled from carriages, free themselves into focus.
Servants alight, carousel on a heel, are gone,
return. A smoked sturgeon the table's length.
Voices. And there a lady
whose knees twitter at the mention of vodka,
an oyster-look about her languor.
There is a centerpiece drifting for our enchantment.
There are playing cards whose flutter to felt
is brighter than numbers. Let us pun
as the tsar passes, gems fogging her throat,
deep gallery of air closing behind her. Let it snow
light zeros beneath the church domes
where the syphilitics, smartly-buttoned, parade out of life—

Listen, we carry what silhouettes we can.
Tonight it is old man Yakovlev,
all Adam's apple, in tango with his latest ghost.
He pretends not to hear me—
Such iridescence my scapegraces,
whose dinner silver cross
their grouse to bits, who lark near walls, stage
a needle's little celebration as it enters,
come and go and return to suck
the loose body of the last stray crayfish—

Come to the downstairs of your life and go
outside— Snowfall, signs latch in the ice.
Each doorway is the precise shape
abandonment would take.
Who sees how beautiful the horses as they wait,
slow and uninterrupted, masters
firelit behind blue windows
and darkening their heads to tipped glasses?
The horses, lantern-jawed, color of stoves,
their outlines steaming peatsmoke,
the sleeping horses who need only
the snow to touch themselves into darkness.

Pygmalion,

Young woman alone,
which is to say witch-hunt's clicking glottis,
madness sash, chosen one for bruised fish,
their stacks radiant as plated rudders.
Which is to say as noon devolves
some pharmaceutical tea, a seagaze.
Summing the coast, the tides gain, gain, undercut the bluffs
and slip their dose over surfaces. And when they retreat
the blue world is blanched white, the rubbed grit of it.
Deep enough, would the palm turn dorsal?
Would I change without tool, stone, without the scarved stool
I rested, astonished by weight and a far quarry reserve?

A falling arc, the ornaments we rip from our throats
fall at precisely the speed their colors call—
were I finning for subdued cracks
shifting with clouds,
hereafter. Were I my life.

Pygmalion,

A cadence that would be sleep as the wafer feathers
the tongue, sea-colors as the light
stains, sea-colors as the stains alight
the vaulted frescoes. Come down, be slight,
skim to me body that is bright life, come down.
How cold the skin of air above stone,
pews bolted, the tomb-pocked floor.
The dead, they come through the floors
shaped as watery bootprints.
In disregard I once held, I the cadence and I the pitch,
come down, be finespun,
sing me lying loose and hymn-crazed in the pew,
lower, undo (o comedy of buttons) massy pearl,
unsheet our matched embrace, parallel collarbones.
Do not leave me. Do not
leave. There is a sea—
veil over nothing, aerialist, touch that untouches itself
as morning comes to glass.

Untitled

Her full dull weight affixed to the boaty accelerator.
Through desert, the gated neighborhoods
smoking emerald, then the city's
pale stone pitching upward.
Where is my dead one she asks.
Here and *here* he points to soil.
A bell, another, then bells—
four-bell peals in the off-and-running noon,
the hour of blue begun of hands
rope to clapper to bowl and nor is it
enough her palms are resting, arrested even,
maybe listening.

Uninflected, unblinking,
Dig her up he says.

Lesser Season (I)

His old tug, the Sea Bull,
falls locked in ice, its smoke red
weathered, drained pink by the stilled river.
Four p.m. moon rise, he hovers,
eclipsing the ice hole, a moon to the moon.
Attentive to trout organs, the delicate
soft-colored globes, he tosses back the insides
except the bladders, which float.
Stacks the fish.
In a year of imperceptible moves
mistaken for silence, he can hear
the static of ice alive,
tinny snaps, a crush of foil
deep in a far hull of his ear—

The drowsy riverpeople point and laugh,
he'll pay in Spring they say.
Mountains hunker under their bluish fur
and light is bound in ice.
Hours of snow return simply, invisibly
appear and fall, how the airless
air takes without him.
He sees the slow plan move tonnage,
winter, from above the ice breaks
on the delta like a fanning stream
of glossy buckshot,
pitches and loosens as bergs,
white bronchial blooms on the sea.

The tug spills its pink wood, a wound
the ice cannot close.
The troutstack like silver kindling.
The ballast has caved, the tug
dying, the ice is dying,
town dogs bounding for a silent frequency,
something to which the deep ear perks.
When the man retrieves the bladders
little rose mouths stain the ice.

The Puppet Shop

Might they be opera people watching a chord
eclipse, be eclipsed. A face adjusts
on its string and another comes
to rest in whatever light winter affords—
so much caution in faces so still, and brief,
the ladies revolving in their gowns
of a single color, gentlemen stitched for elegant
postures to strike at a later hour, waiting
for a handhold to appear in air.
The aproned shopkeeper gestures,
would I like to see one
as the sound of my reach
reaches the doctor's smock, silken cool and white,
spun with luminescence, the kind of sense
only discovered as it escapes—

A nonce Czech word, hard and lyrical, a passing
throat. Stilted shadows
flush to cobble in a mistaken alley. And the stilled saints,
oxidizing dark, each clutching a gold
from some infecting travesty. Even the spires
of this city that lift so clean to the sky,
they plunge, black lances to the static clouds.
Whose hands are these, waiting
for the invisible string? Whose blank face
does the little jig?
Some wind stirs the shaving scents
and the marionettes clack like mad Pinocchios
as the door opens and another fascinated one
steps in, a passenger fresh to his train.
Box the doctor please I say
as I make a shape in the air with my hands—
might I, just one face out of limbo,
the doctor's carved, startled response,
the stitched red cross that pulses his center,
the hands that close against his will

another's eyes, wide, still unsuspecting—
your death, endless, each face
a smaller more perfect doll inside a doll.

Parable

I. Reception

Look at the path the white
pole of light strikes: a lobe, a shoulder
of black mohair, the bow leaning
on the leaning cello.
Without a priest to help us dismantle a thought,
lower a body into the earth,
there is nowhere to pinpoint sadness,
and anything may do: erupted sighs,
the broken bird of the wrist as we cradle
the undersides of wine glasses, poles of light.
Someone recounts the fable of the heron and hunter—
no one can place the story
but everyone remembers when the hunter
glides his caress along the heron, a scene
stamped into a sheet of gold.
Someone coughs, a voice breaks,
odd dents we can't help but to bang
by accident into air.
Silver pins, each through a browning white rose,
its green stem, a patch of black fabric,
glitter breast-high through the room.
In asking how we must first resolve whom—
Perhaps grief begins
a whisper as though we've discovered
a pearl in our mouths, little scene
where the heron is charmed,
abandoning any last clarity of itself,
sinking in the sinking hunter's arms.

II. Burial Procession

In truth the heron will sense
a graceful harm over its life
and lift in one elegant vault.
Waiting for the body to lower,
the family stares at the priest
or into the sea of pressed black clothes.
New white roses with such furious architecture,
the edges spiralling in.
So apparently simple,
like flight or cloud spreading through water,
movement we no longer question.
Still, the family waits,
there is something else entirely—
a bird, a rustle,
the entire flock startled,
each heron shaping into its slicked wing,
hitting the roofless blue.

III. Eulogy

There were no herons and certainly no bird
thinking itself a violent treasure of the sky.
The family grieved itself, a monument
no one visits, and even-pewed spaces

opened between acquaintances,
the body, the priest.
A poem, stories were read.
A delicately dressed man delivered the eulogy.

Perhaps we more often inclined
our heads to smell our roses—
to stay still, the memory
like a finger crowding,
pressing into the breastbone.
Every gesture a match strike
to caution against, this is not us,
we said, not us at all.

For once the empty sky
held its slant, and eyes closed
on imprinted boxes of light,
the outline of good deeds in the stained glass
retreating so slow and plain
we saw how to get older.

Stay still. Who will visit?
Who will come and touch?

Prayer

Of light I am guilty of too much,
cannot help myself, cannot help
how quietly I am overcome: pieces of it now
briefly in play through maples, the leaves carving
up what it can and there I
go again, the bowing shapes, sorrow's flyings,
trees and their governances therein,
the movements of some thoughts as to sea
in a vial, the voiceless to glass,
silence to an edge.
How do I do this? How go
the hands? Inside, a fleetingness
so stationed it is a law: come force and come some unified
exchange, anyone can turn water into air
but who shall return it, the era is loosed,
cities' vast interiors rise and collect more cloud
to reflect, Kalashnikovs spasm into the upper blue,
huge ships list and lower while cathedrals, domes, little huts
antenna for the heavens. Sand has an oceanology
all its own and whatever sweeps across—
heat, distance, blindness—
is dreamy fuel. It pours through windows,
rides under doors, fills open mouths
solid and clear. All is light
and all is the point at which nothing can be said,
is the outcome of glass: exact, transparent, airless.
I have seen the unexpected shape prayer
gives the mouth. Have I? Have
I? I have seen sky.

In the Tattoo Parlor

And having seen have caught the edge of weather
as it moves as it flickers matter:
swordgrass, palm,
all surface lightly scored and by gusts even
what a field of broken sound the bells make
and how chargeless the scraps gulls become—
weather, its lush cusp must be prayer—
a hand touches another's on a shore in a staticky time,
slight shifts of borne-over-sea birds
turn pensive, titanesque,
drag behind into the fabric of air a hole
and in their own time
falter. Expire.
The giving of oneself up
so near indistinct:
the room's pinup lofts, giraffe-like,
the burst on slender ankles if need be
and a high leaf-eating restfulness in her eyes.
There is a sound of which part is difficult to follow—
under it skin fills, blooms,
a hand flown like four hooves removed from earth,
weightless instant of it and mark
on air, hush burning space and light's carriage
in this age our era—   wave, wave
by hoof, wing or water
wave, wave
and in its throat's hollow how easily when swept away
there is still—

how wholly innocent the act of kneeling should appear
so startling, so roofless and hugely
folded—

Lesser Season (II)

As they pass, de-icers, their desperate inertia
frantic as the freshly blind,
touching every surface—
red lights against the falling snow.
This country is full of gravel salts,
lit wooden stars. Stale dynasties
awash with globes of blown glass,
through the center of each a glass
thread, which if heard might sound
as a distant summer:
pine bat to ball,
hammer to lake dock.
Long galloped from the blower's breath, the glass
now cool, a visible trace
to be held in the cathedral
the hands can form.
And no longer a moving wound, the country
loves the snow hours—
scrollwork along bicycle frames, empty laundry lines.
Snow laces the rake teeth,
only the smoking mouths of flues untouched.
Why should we hear beyond the window?
The snow, the snow,
its layers deafening, outlining the pines—
radiant shirtwaists we may not touch.

Northerly

He senses the easy force of horses more privately
in one ear— the iron latches stretching
under weight, slack heavy bursts of air
and a bit of hay turn sheen. Everything is unlightable
portions of horses: the deep inner stifle,
pupils, a nearness to pain so small
it can never be mended. Some racket goes on
from open windows behind him and sounds like irritated wings
trying to settle. To lead the old bay out
into day, to give softly into its graying throat
in one calculated sweep there in the dark dirt
is to become the lone moving part on a stilled earth.

Whatever unfolds from him unfolds
like a neck leaning to clear the next crag.
Through the open stable he can see things move:
the bay in the meadow, the harbor, and running like a current
burning along the distant mast tips, the wind
blooming the flags of countries that week in port.

Lesser Season (III)

Someone stonewatches, can't stamp out
the cold, blows a furnace
into balled hands as the ice storm
slicks the town. The lines are down,
the light rail paralyzed.
Have I looked too much
or hard? Some damage to the hills,
uncroppable fields.

Close up, eyes leap out of fur-lined hoods,
dusty green or blue,
at times opening into shy wilderness.
The man with whey-colored hair
leaning with all his weight on the cane—
looking, relearning.
Not your box-blind, sea-cloud gaze,
the ferocity with which you examined
a locket, or a box so finely wrought
it might hold buttons for a doll—
unapologetic hands,
the box an inch from your face
as if to hear the engraver's work—

At first light, empty, astral plains.
Things ice needled, prismed from a distance.
Even the thinnest ends of the birch stems
gloved in ice, flagpole ropes
englassed, dangerous cable,
a willow chandeliered.
A boy checks the farm well for a slipped trophy buck,
and almost drifts in himself. Nothing down there
but a glossy throat.
How may I even touch my disservice to air,
that indecipherable static—
the entire arctic in sway
to air alive against the walls.

Aloha

And once near I could accordingly become.
Shore as a slim circle of ink. Rushes' curve out the soft shallows,
trout flashes turned surface disturbances
then lake, lake—
skiff's brief knockings, sky, the eye taking pleasure
in whether encompassing or being encompassed.
                                        I wanted to flatten a palm
to the expanse, sense my loosened and drifterly
stay, stay move out over where freely bits of cloud
passed prettily, sun's crossings, air just off water,
air solving a more difficult math there, the lake
antechambered sky, sky
lake, in it the breaking world so as to seem seamless—
that I might grant what arrived unasked-for
stay, and that I, having become, might
accordingly return the world its long-forged self
more exquisitely, more wanted.

The Swords Project

1

Beneath the streets huge wheels are moving
& mammoth birds taking time to lift off estuaries
set their clocks for an hourless dark.
Some say *the face holds its one turn*
yes, yes some say my god they've sharp pieces
up sleeves.
Some are light steps crossing the night
like a field, the feeling of being rumorous among the wheat
turned upon their heads:

2

Children, the coffee is Turkish in a gold-latticed cup.
Children, as we speak the caveat is souring at mouths
passing through the countryside
& the jacquerie is multifronted with streetwaifs like slips of laundry,
breaking open the streets.
Even the king was a boy, practicing his cut & thrust:
hilt, blade, edge, point   one, two, three, four
head, heart, thigh, gut ...
The queen isn't even in the country.
There are hands, children, in them rudely formed glass
& within the glass
the minor skritching of a beetle, nothing so loudly
as the potential of its wings, its spring colors on the move.
So what of fragments into fragments, broken down beyond the eye?
To the king, a life—what is it—

3

Flocks of white spoonbilled birds loft the estuary:
alias on alias on alias.
Some say a snap in the weather can sweeny the horses,
others say grain & all say my dark chestnut   *rest.*
I say the shaking emotion is in the thinking.

4

The birds turn to less beautiful versions of themselves.
The stupid plowing fenders that would touch if asked of them.
A wrong places itself & then is framed against sky.
Hands for, bodies flung, any handhold, for any corridor,
faces holding pattern, crystalline, and who, who can,
of those among this who can hold
smoke & fire, splinters & darken, the scatter & sky,
rain from ceilings saying *try try try,*
everything soon cracking wildly from form, I said soon
it says, I said *now.*
A clutch of air—
Erased from the chest—
Couldn't we fall here? How could we not?
We stand agape at which question?

5

On huge rollers scrapers meant to sway are swaying.
A call, calls, calling …
No one, as pigeons fumble toward glass, to cue the studio laughter.

Project for a Swordfight

So children, do not cha cha
on others when they are down.
And children, do not cry.
Let the class lambs take up blades
to partly inherit the hand that moves through what the others
could not destroy.
Let silence's ambassador, touch,
painful or no, do its thing—
you can never be sure you're hit
until the puffy shirt darkens.

Children, let a sound issue from the throat
& let it, like a single motion, come full—
see the rhythm to the crippled walk?
The swing & throw?

Of the Motion of the Heart and Blood

It is commonly thought the wound is a vow,
     the ushered whisper of, covenant of, the good word of
God moving through the poor unfortunate
     lightened of blood, and unreeling into that constellated
unconscionable color
     says *come back* says *I will heal you* . . .
To the simple man
     directing the great millhorse in the rye-stropped
sweet of dawn, it is commonly thought the circle
     waits to be acted upon, something to plainly fill
or empty— the figged orchard, what the flock free
     of disease can give. Waving before the plow and oxen,
the golden tips, the field whole in its soft score,
     the shush, the occasional floating snap.
And the sky running through his sleeves
     reveals the five wounds of Christ:
One   the left wrist   what will become Destot's space
    Two   the right   Third and Fourth in the
foot's alluvial plain, left over   right
    and Five,   the speartip, gently.
It is uncommon. Gliding the scalloped earth
     such light soil, the instantaneous skies
of September, of heaven and of earth
     held apart by the kind whip falling to rhythm.

The word, *a seeing with one's own eyes.*
     Scalpel, saw, the ashen hue and once
subcutaneous, *triangularis sterni*—
     manubrium, gladiolus, ensiform, it is commonly thought
the sternum is a plate when it is a dagger,
     then the dark and laddered *intercostales* until the ribs crack,
slightly give and fly
     open and like starlings at once from a seeding tree
some shadowed vacuum rushes forth, is met
     by air. *Peri-*
cardium, and within, the only clock I trust—
     the four-chambered heart, of which three is God and one

is man. My good good man I cannot help you now,
      all grounds end in graves, emptied,
slipping the body's locket, slips into
      the sentencing dust where the oxen paw a little,
a voice trailing
      I cannot   *there is too much*   *there is nothing I—*
this boon that does pulse so evenly onto the warm furrows,
      it circles, floats, courses the channels
by the heart directed my good good man
      with mine own eyes I have *seen.*

The Ambulance Came & We Know How That Goes

a hand moves
& is the world
& flaming a little in the detective's grasp
in the light of late fall, the leafed-through flipbook—

                                stray dark strand
                                milligrams
                                the collar flushed (wings)
                                who is this Buzz character?

He says the drug peacefully blinks
one to sleep.   Painless, he says.

(& look, from the Latin, *ambulare,* to walk
though the word as they were dying & they were
dying in trenches.)

So often it is another night & I feel the block
verging on sleep—
a siren reaches its red anchor,
city sounds return.

(With speed Godspeed, Mercí
a shell, the flicked splinter of a shell
& Monsieur have you ever—

                      some blood & the skin heats like a shame.
                          Ambulances volantes. Travelers, flying.)

The hand moves
& is the world
& flaming a little in the hand
the polished instrument vaguely in error & look
a slight ping & the skyscrapers shoot up
overnight like corn. Bullets are loping insects.
How one must work to fly or run
in a dream, the fish
bathypelagic.

(The word made as they were dying,
the wounds under a sunned hand, in it
fresh, white gauze.)

Of visible light, that light cycling for the eye, red is the most languorous wave.
Ambulance. Traveler.

Whose touch is a film, & seamless.
Part for me it says, let me go I have somewhere to go.
All looking is looking for
the dispersing thing—

                      Oh, it is quiet after—

Horses of the Sun (1)

Whether the likeness in the glass part shore, part hand,
part slender stem
is a reciprocity. What is there
and so you turn to touch
some motion in the glass crossing the hardwood
crossed with sun.
These nearnesses press onto us—
the facts that loft through the trees
that are not birds, the drop we think we see
strike the lake and shimmy the reflection.
And permanence?
Water, flower, flesh—
my love, there was something you turned toward to touch.

And whether everything that rises
to a surface, disperses.

Horses of the Sun (2)

And now there is almost no movement.
Air seems lighter
than itself, and the snow from a next earth.
To whom the snow's deep comprehension
of things, to whom this unease
in waking, all still the high, leafy ceilings
and in them birds gone imbecile.
Would I be less afraid in parks on such nights
and on such nights the air of the shallowest
water where huge planed fish part grasses
like a scar. A palm shies before glass—
no motion need now be finished.
Air seems lighter than itself.
Charged nearly,
liquid to touch and though touch be older,
the air is perpetually an air
in which you are about to speak
or about not to speak.

And now very nearly begins
the division of trees—
my love, to move out from under is all we have.
And now to wake eyes skyward in some terrible
stance of the body
is all we have.

Horses of the Sun (3)

So many of the near poor here
whose motion is accommodated, made beautiful even
by evening slightly massing under the trees,
by the blonde grasses bowing, all silent permission
and surface, soon voices, soon rising out of the burned places
the wending alleyway women, deep bass knuckling
toward the walls and the young pulled away
from windows. How long the brief piece of curtain once disturbed
takes to settle.

Evening and the whole block yawns
into gulf. *I feel afraid* she says
and I feel a dream's vague recurrence of
a pack of something light popping
in the chest. Cannot evening become
anything other than so many mouthings behind glass—
the poor who robe themselves
in light's thinnest imaginable paper, trees
the color of shrapnel, trees they
squander electric light.
A patrol floats through.
Someone forces a thumb over a dog's mouth.

Involuntary the chest—small, pinned, a fact
nearly.
All study of shot children,
the movements of their hands,
confirms a flower bloom is in crises.
I feel afraid / what's slight of mass / the light
changes just now and is so—
what is
is not beautiful and yet is—

Horses of the Sun (4)

Clymene: It is given to none of us to behold them—the bright horses of the sun.

Apollo: You cannot bridle their pull, nor, mind you, what they pull.

Phaeton: I said give me the reins.

Horses of the Sun (5)

I.

That *a line is breadthless length*
is what calms, that I may replace force
with almost sea or sealight along the line's span,
the makeshift distance, that I then am the point
moving through that wide hush—
I feel wind throw clear light
from my throat, feel the O
spread through women and children,
air turn flame and a young hand go up.
Smoke falls on voices. Movements,
they collectively sound as nothing
falling all around. Static floats.
Who can see so small
that part which takes, at what point
air, at what
fire? Whether I say
something of grace, a thing or two of
concession, within opens still
within—
what is there.

II.

And I saw that a horse had broken its rein
in the brassy plains of a windy age.
Clouds foamed from an edge. Whomever   (a boy)
opened the stable's door was pardoned— nothing
could look out on so much hush and not want.
Fields waved, through which a line shone with no end.
Every "here"
became
here.

44

Horses of the Sun (6)

This is the land of others unleashing upon the world.
Entire wrongheaded lives play out. Transparency pushes for lakefloor.
Where what gleams reveals itself so openly
and selfless we cannot help but laugh and throw
our hands up. Where we are of sense,
the one just so of timing and chests
stolen of air—that justice
of small winds, incongruencies in touch, occasional
sorrow.

Horses of the Sun (7)

In the small air we let slip our mouths—
In the sound without turn, and brief
the parted mouth whose slip between—
How are our mouths so bared by a word,
its current quieting
noise, the clicking of trash—
In a word comes a deep fullness of light
people in the streets seem to rise toward.
Light carries across the mirrored scrapers,
glass fields the birds skim,
light meant for us to see
the wing's verge, sky, to catch the atom's slide
into the other, to say
there is feather and *there*
is air.

Because I cannot make certain the world's assembling
of things, how deeply an object is itself,
what passes becomes less praised, missed nearly—
The afterlull of some surface, electric tints there,
the pre-storm center of a field
and so on until my hand
opens for any stranger who would have it.
Even in the free afternoons of the cool museums
the guards, with the wave of a hand, say I must not breathe
so close.
In my breath.   *Which would hurt the color.*   *Something living.*

The living
cannot make for certain. The living
of blood, bone, of tissue and spark,
mere crux, of occurrence, of the body
brief in what it's given, hands
moving over collars open at the neck,
hands fielding machines, irrepressible that lean
into machines, faces into likenesses of birds or sand,

the living living like draft horses
and the poor openly in the streets.
Mouths of us all shaping certain words
to which some eyes are a vastness, something felled
in us, to which some announce failures skyward—
do not look away
we insist and hold the other's eyes
open in love.

I thought I had come to know the light called forward
by horses of the sun.
I thought to see was to feel; thought could be
no more a permanence than touch, the voice that in a word
rises into matter.
Voices, touch. So many shades of former voices, touch.
And permanence?—
My love, there was something you turned toward to touch—
Such a small weight
your parted hand resting
on my chest.

Easterly

See the living held-at-arm's length from the living.
So unharmed they wait, the belief that children
wander so they will never wander.
The sailor still, having cut away in thought—
no need here for rope in hand, hard tack.
See the wing enter, see it come off the sea,
allowing just so to happen, that
Who are you a sound arriving
in the shape of a bell.

From broken boxes the iron shot spills,
the hull pitches, windless parachutes
touch the dusky decks of gold and wood
which flood to black—
some have always imagined themselves
canopies of sail
falling darkly through deeper waters.

Lure

1

Nearly wasted now, earth's curve—
is it the radio's thin transmission that tethers,
could we not go higher until it is unclear
(Egypt nine nine zero good evening)
which properties things possess, yes, the cockpit glass
could simply step out
of its dress. It will be unclear and attend on us,
the voice from a stray headset louder
when it should be faint, should we answer for the passengers
sleeping or for the passengers, heads into knees,
mistaken for sleep. Should we,
as though of a pull of mirrors, flare
then quiet before the instruments lose
their symmetry, and siren, and hands pull
deerlunged at the gauges.
Captain, we are so far from that blue—
a body is a bright soundless suspense through the clear
(Egypt nine nine zero you are clear),
until that body wakes sir, finds itself in the place
it thought it was meant to be.

2

The diamond like a seagreen fan opened
and rested on the desert floor.
Heat rises the mowed outfields. Boys groom the basepaths.
They have taken the field, professionals
shaped from the cooled interiors of 600SLs,
they have taken the field from which three birds lifted.
                    (Are you a pigeon a dove?)
Do you see how grace will not wave away—
a girl sweeps into the box full of bright ices,
as she leans her Love-in-Tokyos
two condensed sirens briefly aflare.
                    (A mourning dove. Ash-white, spearing shade to shade.)
Come, lift now, there is no other way—
the storked left-hander sails into windmill,
gloves flex, cleats rise,
one imagines sound carry one imagines
the sea, kite-thin, aboard this field,
the ball sunfused, reclining on a line as it nears.
Flightpath.   (Some heat ushering off your spread wing.)
What grace allows—
the baseball simply drifts right through,
brief white cloud,
a dress strap slips from a bare shoulder.

3

Which is to say inherit the earth.
Which is the desert deserting itself,
the sea a child fluttery on aspirin.
This mountain station a wing too close to a sun.
We've evacuated the sky.
A plume rises into the radio layer.
We've evacuated the lakes. Some part of us
wants to concede, "Mr. President, we're sorry,
Mr. President, there will be a terrible
cloud." But it's just Harry. He won't budge, the radio skips
and I listen, only a Richter quietly
etching in a far bright lab.
Persuading, always persuading,
the wind, and why try anyway when it only makes the hand
gesturing "stop" more handish, petty,
and moves on
rippling over the lake like a curtain that fills
though the window is tight—
last charged breath called mercy. The mountain will loosen,
mercy,
float apart in blocks, listen,
for longer stretches the lake so stationary, a jewelled lung.
A swan tears at underwater grasses.

4 The Lady of Matchboxes (A Narrative)

The Lady of Matchboxes has a full set of teeth,
she dreams them never kicked in, nor soft-
tinted bulbs that flower into nettle.
Bits of tooth never crumble her throat.
So early the center of the city is never
so singular— distant traffic thickening at the bridge,
a scarf to wind, her cards pressed open
face to the sidewalk, waiting.
Do the first suits, unhorsed from metro holes, see her?
Once she was an albatross at such height
she found the movements of troops beautiful,
that series of circles ever tightening until night fires
littered only one valley.
Wild iron flashed, delayed booms.
So many pistols hidden at hemlines!
Do they see her ... no one sees her.
They transfix by, though some have hands
she sees them by, some fisted, some palming
air, that difference between sensing,
something in anticipation of sensing.
Close your eyes say the hands,
it is raining,
close your eyes they say,
it is about to rain ...

5

I've pressed her a bill I've folded and blown myself into
and she has touched my palm and I an unseen card,
rolled the bony die near the stale empty fifths like sighs of wreckage
guarding the near and sleeping drunks, the drunks lights-out
on stoops

6 The Card

and a woman exits
the rail, a red dress, a man
in a flecked suit rushing arms outstretched.
Arches lifted, she is just taking leave,
a cool blink and one hand as if accepting an hors d'oeuvre
in air—
Suicide at Sea, longed for
yes—

                      Never to be found,
but was this not choice,
never found, unfounded—
the rail is leaving her, she has a red dress.

7 Weather

                Then quiet then
snow, then
leafy maples, snowstrung.
To whom this night   the unchecked hours
to whom the white woven glow
clipping the early gardens.
To whom this pleasure of
waking.

             They float apart,
sound of this
as the maples—
flimsy go
their proud outlines, the snow a spike driving the center
from above.

And the sleek cars,
bass shaking snow, wish

                    to pass close.
Whose honks wake us,
who see a ceiling under which a bright lane hums
and laugh, apply
lipstick, accelerate.
Who wish to go toe-to-toe,
             the high school daughters
in deep cars.

             Do you think yourself
into something
my love,
or does there simply appear a spotless window,
a stunned dovelet?
             And yet
Look!
      Without a scratch, the snow—

8

Captain, nobody could say I know nothing
of you—
in Cairo a daughter is ill.
How you said two creams, yes two creams and one sugar—
right eye swayed, manic, the disc in the left
threaded, pooling its dish.
Oval of your mouth diminishing.
Captain, some sleep, timed by the easy engines,
all would sleep if they took by force the light
rinsing the cockpit. Its half-shell returns
a shape, a face, guages under palms
now calm like burnt districts cooling,
air made up of remote, releasing things.
We have no camel roped to the stake on this one—
you said this yourself, the door clicked
and there was Adel.
You said Adel, what's with you,
why did you get all dressed in red like that?
Nobody could answer,   black box whirring,
Adel as if he'd sky off the plane's deck
and I felt an idea of water so beautiful then and only then—
of two rooms, of someone, hand at the glass, watching
how easily when soundproof
the ribs crack open, like clearing dried brush,
how easy to reach the heart.

The sea will rip through us.
Through bodies as falls apart soaked bread.
You see we have no camel,
just wave-palmed mirages, glassy feeders, a sculpted dune.
Captain, at contact we touch into elsewhere—
so many sleep, some with a clarvoyance so brash
I cannot help but love—
the radio, the radio skipping like a girl
in Ohio—
a daughter ill, this I know, sir, of you.
Even a body of light drops silent and sky deep

into a damaged ear, mistaken for a sound
of water parting, an ocean stilling
behind glass, there, someone
with a hand to its surface, watching.

9 The Lady of Matchboxes Dreams An Albatross in a Barn

Still, so still the machines.
An inverted till, the air trained
electric at the graze of a wing—
something miscaged and drugged; I should have known
an evening composed
entirely of heartskips—
what a night O what an alarmed lark
of a night, O what
a *Why Here?*
Silhouette of pipes and claws, draped things,
the day let down as
soft iridescent oils loft to surfaces—
something clipped.
Should have known an evening would end like this.
O what
a once in love
that has not yet thought to press an ear to its ceiling.
Too still, and winglocked, so much metal
like lakewater, and snagged,
a feather torn on a cracked plow-wing,
the fresh sting risen to a single
vermilion disc. What a thing to match colors
in the eyes, or when none,
what a color
for something aflutter in a drum.
Should have known the evening is pillowtalk,
'night love, 'night love, then night:
                    how simple a movement until
it must be ours.

10

What it does or doesn't.
The air simply parts before it.
The red seam cannot forgive
on account of its own
mathematics and its appearing so wounded.
There isn't even a clock to fight against.
How soft the follow-through—
flightpath.
How few fathom anything done near quiet—
flightpath.
Pray, don't move so and so,
or do, for what espouses, what simply sidesteps
is the same and why
look back.
Please
it is simply not true we have grown
so estranged from matter, matter
from us.

11

The serenade an almost-nothing, a kind of listening:

ha la
ha la   la lei

Replacing lakewater with a face,
the wind, simply, as a wish
does the morning unwindings—
Its blur moves the lake's length.
Mr. President, chin up. Chin up,
what comes accepts nothing from us,
its beauty heavy in having the poplars
turn glitter, and snap—

ha la lei
ha lei la
hey hey la lei   la la

One listens for the other
on a radio channel left open,
a deskchair rolling on linoleum, some papers shuffled
low and in waves for when no others will come to this place—
the wind's moved on and Harry,
you're cabin's lost in the lake's glare.

hey ha hey ha
hey ha ha

The radio, the radio
goes shhh shhh shhh shhh—
Somewhere last night,
tracing the seam of a baseball and nearing sleep,
a boy.
Vancouver, Vancouver   this
is it.

12 The Lady of Matchboxes (Blank Card)

The suicide try is all over the afternoon edition:
there is a lone figure on the downturned glance
of bridgesteel, a long dark brick of traffic,
the bay, fluttery ...
What can I say that hasn't and what
do I think I am that simply replaces
what you see with what you do not
even know is absent—
My lady, the blank card is glass
and the barn window.
Depending on the light, a face reflects
the soft weather of lines.
Depending on the light, the beyond,
your paramour, his glides ghostly, extended.
And depending on the light at evening
one so nearly transposed on the other
the difference vanishes—
evening, the suicide has the ill speaking
things beautiful, have so many of us
awkward for them, leaning with tablets or coins.
Illuminated, flouncy clouds,
wind died down,
the city gone to dinner tables and your
                              fortune, fortune sir
as they pass. My lady, your heart skips—
things beautiful not because fleeting,
things beautiful because they are to come and have long
been poised so.

13

The still-to-learn, the unheard-of, the haven't-you-known
all in place and buckled, eyes closed.
A pure undinted light bluing at contact
and how lovely the semicircle's motion, earth's curve vanished.

Captain, yes, the engines are shut.

Of habits, the ghostlier one of placing ourselves
for the taking— the eyes so unconsciously
falling on this or that or whatever pleasing just then.
The comatose ... someone forces the eyes wide open—
nothing.
How many times until we are not surprised?

Captain, I rely on God.
(Egypt nine nine zero respond)
Captain, I place myself in the hands of God.

And how many times until we are not surprised,
the eyes' unaccountable color, freshets of color—
we give in, we cave, offer ourselves up
to what we feel we see,
eyes closed, head placed in the easy curve
of knees ready to receive—

Captain, I rely on God.
(Egypt nine ninety if you copy)
Captain, sleeping, I go to God.

Swimming in the sea and a light felt close.
Swimming in the sea and the soft dark disc centers itself.

Notes

Westerly, Southerly, Northerly, Easterly:

On Sunday, August 10, 1628, the Vasa, the largest warship of its time, went down on its maiden sail, never having left the Stockholm harbor. The ship was salvaged in its near entirety in the 1960's, and now rests in a Stockholm museum as the world's only 17th century warship on display.

Revolving Around Tycho Brahe: Wenceslas Square:

Tycho Brahe (1546-1601), Danish astronomer who believed the sun revolved around the Earth. He is buried in the Tyn Church in Prague.

Stradivari, 1736:

Antonius Stradivari (1644-1737), master Luthier, produced the Countess of Stanlein, his last cello, in 1736. There is speculation as to how much Carlos Bergonzi (1683-1747) helped Stradivari in his later years. From Stradivari's workshop there was a direct line of sight to the inner recesses of the Basilica of San Domenico, where Stradivari was buried, though the church was later destroyed, rendering the whereabouts of Stradivari's remains unknown.

Diodic:

Joseph Severn (1793-1897), English portrait and landscape painter, who was at Keats' side when he died in Rome on February 23, 1821.

Desperation Series:

Contains references to Katie Ford's "Last Breath and Diseases in the Wheat" and Robert Frost's "The Most of It."

The Stone Letters:

Catherine the Great (1729-1796).

Postnik Yakovlev, architect of the St. Basil's Cathedral in the Kremlin. Ivan IV allegedly had Yakovlev's eyes removed so that he would not create another as beautiful.

Of the Motion of the Heart and Blood:

William Harvey (1578-1657), Jacobean anatomist and scientist, wrote *Of the Motion of the Heart and Blood in Animals* in 1628, postulating for the first time that blood was circulated through the body by the heart, and not by some pulsing action of the arteries.

Horses of the Sun:

(4) "It is given to none of us to behold them—the bright horses of the sun," is attributed to David Wilson-Okamura's translation of the *Aeneid.*

(5) "A line is breadthless length," is attributed to Thomas Heath's translation of Euclid.

On December 30, 1903, the Iroquois Theatre in Chicago erupted in flames, killing at least 600 people, mostly women and children. Of the more than 500 performers, only the tightrope artist perished, caught high above the scene.

(7) Greatly influenced by George Oppen's "A Narrative."

Lure:

October 31, 1999: Egypt Flight 990 crashes into the Atlantic, killing 217. After extensive research, the consensus of the National Transportation Safety Board is that one of the co-pilots took the plane down, although there are many existing theories, conspiratorial and otherwise. Portions of the poem are excerpted from the cockpit transcript.

March 26, 2001: In spring training, a Randy Johnson fastball collides with a mourning dove, killing the bird instantly.

May 18, 1980, 8:32 AM: Mt. St. Helens erupts, killing 57, including David Johnston, a volcanologist stationed 5 miles from the blast. The eruption also kills Spirit Lake resident Harry Truman, who refused to leave his cabin. Mr. Truman's resolve reminded some of the former President of the United States. The poem also contains the last transmission from David Johnston.